EVERYBODY'S REVOLUTION

A New Look at the People
Who Won America's Freedom

THOMAS FLEMING

SCHOLASTIC NONFICTION

An imprint of

SCHOLASTIC

New York Toronto London Auckland Sydney
Mexico City New Delhi Hong Kong Buenos Aires

To my grandchildren, Noah, Kathryn, Helen,
Lucie, Pauline, Madeleine, and John —T.F.

IMAGE SOURCE NOTES: Pages 1, 4, 7, 9, 10, 13, 14, 16, 18, 20, 23, 24, 26, 27, 28, 29, 31, 32, 36, 38, 40, 42, 43, 44, 50, 53, 54, 56, 58, 63, 64, 69, 70, 72, 75, 76, 78, 79, 80, 82, 86, 88, 90–91, 92: The Granger Collection, New York; Pages 6, 34, 39, 61, 66: Library of Congress; Page 8: Bettmann/CORBIS; Page 17: NARA; Page 19: Photo courtesy of Military and Historical Image Bank; Page 21: Collection of the Martin Art Gallery, Muhlenberg College, Allentown, Pennsylvania; Page 46: Courtesy of David R. Wagner; Page 49: University of Georgia Libraries; Page 65: Miriam and Ira D. Wallach Division of Art, The New York Public Library; Page 84: State of South Carolina.

ISBN-13: 978-0-545-01974-3
ISBN-10: 0-545-01974-5

12 11 10 9 8 7 6 5 4 3 2 1   8 9 10 11 12/0

Printed in the U.S.A.   08
First Scholastic paperback printing, March 2008
Book design by Nancy Sabato

CONTENTS

WHAT DOES THE AMERICAN REVOLUTION HAVE TO DO WITH ME?

That was my reaction when I started reading about it at the age of twelve. I got the impression that the war was a struggle between two groups of Englishmen who happened to live on opposite sides of the Atlantic Ocean. I felt left out of the story. All four of my grandparents had been born in Ireland.

When I talked it over with my friends, I found a lot of them felt the same way. Almost all of their parents or grandparents came from Ireland or Italy or Germany or other countries on the European mainland. None of us felt connected to the Revolution.

On April 19, 1775, six companies of British light infantry opened fire on seventy militiamen gathered on the Lexington, Massachusetts, two-acre common. The militiamen, who had resolved "not to meddle" with the British, fired back. Eight Americans were killed, ten wounded. The Revolutionary War had begun.

When I grew up and started doing serious research in American history, I realized that this first impression was wrong. The Revolution was not fought and won exclusively by Americans of English descent. Men and women from a startling variety of countries and races played leading roles in the eight-year struggle for independence. My youthful friends and I had a stake in it after all.

I discovered that Revolutionary America was almost as diverse as the United States is today. When the Revolution began in 1775, the English colonies in North America were more than 150 years old. In the course of those fifteen decades, the original English settlers had been joined by tens of thousands of immigrants from other parts of the world. Approximately 40 percent of the colonists — two people out of every five — were Irish, Scottish, German, Jewish, Dutch, Swedish, Polish, French, Swiss, or African.

Did they all participate in the Revolution? You bet they did! That is why reading this book

This illustration of a chopped-up snake was published by Benjamin Franklin in his newspaper, *The Pennsylvania Gazette*, in 1754. He was urging the thirteen American colonies to unite against the French. The same cartoon was equally good advice during the American Revolution, twenty years later.

almost as diverse as the United States is today.

When news of the Declaration of Independence reached New York City on July 9, 1776, protestors known as the Sons of Liberty pulled down a huge statue of King George III on horseback. One of the leaders of the Sons of Liberty was the Scottish-born son of a milkman, Alexander McDougall.

will be a very important part of your education. It will tell you something most people still do not know about the epic struggle that created our unique country.

Today's Americans value diversity. We are proud that anyone can become an American, no matter what his or her race or ethnic background may be. It has not always been this way. The United States has gone through periods when African Americans, women, and Native Americans were considered inferior and immigrants were likely to meet dislike and even hostility. In some parts of the country, these attitudes can still be found. One reason for the prejudice is a distorted view of the American Revolution.

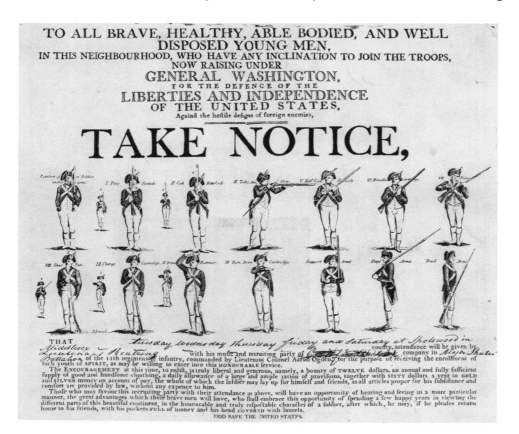

This recruiting poster was distributed throughout the thirteen colonies to encourage men to join George Washington's Continental army. The soldiers promised to serve for three years or the duration of the war. The drawings show a soldier performing the drill in handling a musket.

Dramatic evidence of the diversity — and courage — of the men and women of 1775 was visible from the start of the struggle with England. When the Continental Congress issued the Declaration of Independence in 1776, fifty-six men, who had been chosen to represent the thirteen English colonies along the Atlantic seaboard from Massachusetts to Georgia, signed it.

By doing so, these men risked their lives. To revolt against the rule of George III, the king of England, was treason, and the penalty for treason was death. Eighteen of the signers of the Declaration of Independence were not English. Eight were first-generation immigrants. Can anyone ask for better proof of how many leaders had already emerged among people from non-English lands?

I think you'll be amazed, as I was, by the sheer number of non-English Americans who joined the war as fighting men — and women. Historians now estimate that

In 1765, the British made their first attempt to tax Americans. The Stamp Act required them to buy official stamps for legal documents, newspapers, licenses, even for playing cards. Americans protested violently. Here we see New Yorkers taking to the streets crying "No taxation without representation!"

French Allies **The Revolution became a world war when France signed an alliance with the United States in 1778. In this picture, a young French nobleman is saying farewell to his tearful family to go to America to fight for liberty.**

one-third of the American regular army — usually called the "Continental" army — was Irish-born or of Irish ancestry.

Another 20 percent were German Americans. Germans were as numerous as the Irish in the thirteen rebellious colonies and were equally passionate defenders of their new country.

Hundreds of Dutch names also appear on the rolls of the Continental army. In 1664, the English conquered the Dutch colony of New Netherlands and renamed it New York. However, tens of thousands of Dutch remained in America and became enthusiastic revolutionaries.

Fewer in number, French Protestants driven from Catholic France by religious persecution were influential supporters of independence. They were called Huguenots, after a gate in the

French city of Tours, where they used to meet secretly to elude their persecutors.

During the Revolution, Huguenot leaders welcomed the numerous Catholic army officers from France who joined the American army as volunteers. The struggle for liberty took precedence over old religious feuds.

The first Jews came to America in 1654, fleeing religious persecution in Spain. By the time the Revolution began there were Jewish communities in a half dozen seaboard cities, including Philadelphia, Newport, Charleston, and Savannah. Many of their men joined the fight for independence as soldiers. Others devoted their abilities as businessmen to financing the long struggle for freedom. Though their numbers were small — about 2,500 — they were passionate supporters of the Declaration's call for liberty and equality.

Far more numerous was another group of men and women who seemed at first glance to have no stake in a war for freedom and equality. Almost all of the hundreds of thousands of African Americans in the thirteen rebelling colonies were slaves when the Revolution began. In spite of this harsh fact, thousands of them participated in the struggle. By 1780, one out of every seven men in General Washington's army was black.

Even less well known are the Indian warriors who fought beside the Americans in many battles. Several won commissions in the American army. Not until the twenty-first century did we learn about these forgotten sons of liberty.

For generations, historians also ignored the part that American women played in the Revolution. I was amazed to discover that several women saw combat. Hundreds more assisted the troops as nurses, cooks, and laundresses.

Some especially daring women risked spying on the British. One secret agent warned **George Washington** about an enemy plan that would have wrecked American hopes for victory. Tens of thousands of other women endured loneliness and hardship while their men fought the battles.

Most forgotten of all are the young boys and girls who joined the struggle. You will be fascinated by some of the things they did on and off the battlefields. The war changed their teenage years as much as it transformed their parents' lives.

All these defiant Americans were determined to establish a nation where they would be free to speak their minds, to worship as they pleased, and to own their own land. They also wanted to decide how — and by whom — they would be governed.

Not all these seekers achieved their goals by the end of the war. Some had to wait decades to become full participants in this new land of liberty. Still, when we look back at their stories, we can see that the roots of their eventual liberation were planted in 1776.

This new way of viewing the war for independence adds an inspiring dimension to the drama. Across the gap of more than two centuries, the men and women of 1776 have a message for modern Americans. The American Revolution was everybody's revolution. Today, it belongs to all of us.

The decision to revolt against England was debated throughout the colonies. Women participated in many of these discussions. Here a young woman listens to what her town's elders are saying about the upheaval.

CHAPTER ONE

LEADERS FROM MANY LANDS

"Give me liberty or give me death!" shouted **Patrick Henry** to the members of the Virginia Assembly as they debated how to respond to British threats. His words became the first great war cry of the American Revolution. A year later, this backwoods lawyer was elected governor of Virginia, the largest state in the new American union.

Patrick Henry's ascent to power and influence is typical of the way leaders emerged from non-English ethnic groups. Even before the Revolution began, America was a free society. Everyone had the right to speak out boldly and say what he or she pleased.

When the Virginia Assembly hesitated to put the colony on a war footing in 1775, Patrick Henry gave a fiery speech. "If we wish to be free, we must fight!" he shouted. "I know not what course others may take, but as for me, give me liberty or give me death!" Many delegates thought he was going too far.

Henry was descended from Scottish Presbyterians who had settled in Virginia's backcountry. They had brought with them from their homeland a profound suspicion of British rule. For centuries Britain had oppressed the Scots and crushed their attempts to win independence.

That undoubtedly explains why Patrick Henry's fellow Scottish Americans were well represented in the Revolutionary ranks. Perhaps their best-known warrior was John Paul Jones, a naval hero who was born in 1747 in Kirkcudbrightshire, Scotland. In 1779,

In Virginia and elsewhere, taverns became "nurseries of the Revolution." Here, five of Virginia's leaders plot political strategy at the Raleigh Tavern in Williamsburg.

the slim, hot-tempered Jones commanded a five-warship flotilla that circled the British Isles, capturing seventeen merchant ships. He capped this performance by defeating the British man-of-war HMS *Serapis* off the English coast, while thousands of dismayed Englishmen watched from the shore.

Another bold Scot, beefy bookseller **Henry Knox**, fought as a volunteer at the 1775 battle of Bunker Hill. A few weeks later, General Washington met Knox in Cambridge and was so impressed with his military knowledge that he asked him to join his headquarters staff.

Commodore John Paul Jones (*far right*) was one of the ablest of the many Scots who fought for America. In mid-August 1779, he won a fierce moonlit battle off the British coast with the Royal Navy frigate HMS *Serapis*. Men from eleven different nations were in Jones's crew.

General Henry Knox, commander of American artillery, was a Scot whose family came to America by way of Ireland. He was among the first to call George Washington "the father of his country."

The American army was desperately short of cannons. In the winter of 1776, Knox organized teams of men and oxen that hauled more than sixty heavy guns from Fort Ticonderoga in upstate New York to Boston, a three-hundred-mile journey up and down the steep, snowy slopes of the Berkshire Mountains. Some of the guns weighed more than a ton. Washington used the cannons to drive the British out of Boston. Knox soon became chief of artillery in the Continental army.

THE IRISH WERE NOT FAR BEHIND THE SCOTS IN TERMS of boldness. John Sullivan of New Hampshire was the son of a schoolteacher from Ireland's county Limerick. In December 1774, four months before the shooting war began, Sullivan learned that the British planned to station a regiment at Fort William and Mary in Portsmouth, New Hampshire's capital, to intimidate the patriots.

Sullivan led a raid on the fort early the next day. His men overwhelmed the small British garrison, hauled down the flag, and carried off one hundred barrels of gunpowder. Some of that powder was used with deadly effect six months later at the battle of Bunker Hill. Sullivan was soon a major general in Washington's army. After the war, he became governor of New Hampshire.

Another Irishman — in fact, a whole family of them — struck the first blow against the English on the sea. In May 1775, a month after the battles of Lexington and Concord, the British sloop-of-war HMS *Margaretta* entered Machias Bay, Maine, home of **Maurice O'Brien** and his five sons. The O'Briens organized a group of local fishermen, who put to sea in their boats and captured the befuddled British sailors by boarding them in a wild rush. In Boston, the infuriated English admiral sent two more sloops north to regain the *Margaretta*. The salty O'Briens and their neighbors captured them, too.

Probably the most famous Irish American leader was **Charles Carroll** of Maryland. Writing under the pen name "First Citizen," he persuaded Maryland to join the Revolution.

This Irish-made drum may have been used to summon militia to battle in an emergency. Militia were part-time soldiers. Drumbeats were also used to give orders on a battlefield.

Charles Carroll was the leading Irish American of 1776. His family's experience with British oppression in Ireland persuaded him to sign the Declaration of Independence without the slightest hesitation.

Carroll was educated in France by his wealthy father and came home to become the richest man in America by 1776. Carroll knew he was risking a death sentence for treason and the confiscation of his wealth if America lost the war. Yet Carroll did not hesitate to sign the Declaration of Independence. He took the risk because he knew from his family's experience in Ireland what would happen if Britain was allowed to oppress America with taxes and laws passed by a parliament in which America did not have a single representative. Americans would have been as ruthlessly exploited as the Irish were in Ireland.

Less well known is the story of a working-class Irishman, cheerful, outspoken Hercules Mulligan. He shocked his American friends by welcoming the redcoats — British regiments — when they captured New York in 1776. A skilled tailor, Mulligan was soon making money outfitting British officers and wealthy Americans who had remained loyal to the king.

Even outside of New York City, Americans shook their heads.

Who could believe Mulligan had become a traitor? He had seemed to be a fervent patriot. Mulligan still was, but only a few people knew it. One of these insiders was General George Washington. Another was Washington's aide-de-camp, Lieutenant Colonel **Alexander Hamilton**, who was a close friend of Mulligan's. Throughout the war, the Irishman was one of America's most valuable spies. Among other things, he warned Washington of a well-organized British plot to kidnap him.

At the end of the war, the British evacuated New York. Quite a few American hotheads vowed that they would make Mulligan sorry for his treachery. Imagine their surprise when General Washington rode into the city at the head of his troops and announced that the following morning he planned to have breakfast with his friend Hercules Mulligan.

ONE OF THE MOST PASSIONATE GERMAN AMERICAN LEADERS OF the fight for liberty was **Peter Muhlenberg**, the pastor of a Lutheran church in Virginia's Shenandoah Valley. In January 1776, he stirred his German immigrant congregation with a fiery sermon.

Peter Muhlenberg **was a spokesman for German Americans. A Lutheran minister, he was a major general in the Revolution and served as a congressman and U.S. senator from Pennsylvania after the war. He was a brilliant orator.**

"There is a time for preaching and praying," he told them, "but also a time for battle; and that time has now arrived."

Flinging aside his clerical robes, Muhlenberg revealed the uniform of an American colonel. Three hundred men from his congregation enlisted at the church door. By 1777, the pastor had become a brigadier general.

Stocky, pipe-smoking **Nicholas Herkimer** of upstate New York was also a fervent independence man. When the war began, Herkimer organized four regiments. They were all commanded by German colonels, and most of the recruits were German as well. In 1777, when British strategy called for splitting the colonies in half by subduing New York State and controlling the Hudson River, General Herkimer was the first to upset their plan.

In a fierce encounter at Oriskany in the Mohawk Valley, Herkimer fought his way out of an ambush. Although mortally wounded, he directed an all-day battle that drove back the British and their Indian allies, inflicting heavy losses. It was a crucial victory that soon led to the British defeat at the battle of Saratoga, a turning point in the war.

German American General Nicholas Herkimer and his mostly German followers helped stop the 1777 British invasion of New York. At Oriskany in the Mohawk Valley, he fought Iroquois Indians and loyalist Americans to a bloody standstill. Herkimer died of complications from a leg wound a few days after the battle.

West Point and other military academies still follow Steuben's teachings.

Baron Friedrich Wilhelm von Steuben was probably the best-known German in the American Revolution. A burly, good-natured man, Steuben was a former Prussian officer who took charge of General Washington's demoralized soldiers at Valley Forge and turned them into a professional army. He amazed American officers by personally drilling the men on the parade ground. Until Steuben arrived, the officers left this task to sergeants, as in the English army.

Steuben also wrote a book, carefully describing the duties of each officer. Perhaps most important were his instructions for a captain. "His first object should be to gain the love of his men, by treating them with all possible kindness and humanity." West Point and other military academies still follow Steuben's teachings.

BOSTONIAN **Paul Revere**, THE SILVERSMITH WHO SPREAD THE ALARM THAT triggered armed resistance in Massachusetts on April 19, 1775, was the son of a French Protestant immigrant named Apollos de Revoire. Few could match Revere's endurance and daring. Earlier, in 1774, he rode virtually nonstop from Boston to Philadelphia with important information for the Massachusetts delegates

Here an artist portrays Washington with some of the leading foreign officers in the American army, including German-born Johann de Kalb and Friedrich von Steuben, and two Poles, Casimir Pulaski and Thaddeus Kosciuszko.

THE MIDNIGHT RIDE OF PAUL REVERE.

Paul Revere, son of a French Protestant immigrant, triggered the shooting war on April 19, 1775, when he warned the minutemen of Massachusetts that the British were marching from Boston to seize American gunpowder in Concord.

to the First Continental Congress. He also rode to Portsmouth, New Hampshire, to warn John Sullivan of the British plan to station a regiment there.

On the night of April 18, 1775, Revere was ordered to warn American leaders in Concord that the British were sending 750 men to seize the colony of Massachusetts's supply of gunpowder. He eluded British sentries and was soon on a powerful mare, alerting Concord, Lexington, and other towns of the coming invasion.

Captured on the road by a British patrol, Revere did not even blink when a major put a pistol to his head and ordered him to tell the truth or he would blow out his brains. Revere coolly informed the major that he had "alarmed the country all the way up" and five hundred men were gathering to confront the British. The rattled major eventually let Revere go and hastily retreated to Boston. A few hours later, the Americans and the British exchanged gunfire on the green at Lexington, starting the Revolutionary War.

Another patriot of French Huguenot ancestry,

In 1775, this handbill lists some of the names of the 49 colonists killed and 39 wounded at the battles of Lexington and Concord. The British lost 73 and 174 were wounded.

President of the Continental Congress Henry Laurens of South Carolina was descended from French Protestants. He helped defend Washington against attacks on his leadership during the Valley Forge winter.

Henry Laurens of South Carolina, served as president of the Continental Congress in 1777–1778. This was an extremely important job — the closest thing the Revolutionists had to a national political leader. In 1778, while the American army endured cold and hunger at Valley Forge, President Laurens discovered that a group of disgruntled congressmen and army officers were trying to force General Washington to resign as commander in chief. Laurens told his son, John, who was serving as one of Washington's aides. Together they helped Washington outwit the plotters. Some historians consider this moment an unrecognized turning point in the Revolution.

Probably the most distinguished Revolutionary leader of French Huguenot descent was New York's John Jay. Some historians call him "the forgotten founding father." He was a brilliant lawyer, a master diplomat, and a shrewd politician. He wrote the constitution for New York State in 1777 and became the state's first chief justice. He served as president of the Continental

Congress in late 1778. A year later he was appointed ambassador to Spain, and in 1782, he joined John Adams and Benjamin Franklin in Paris to negotiate the treaty of peace with England.

Back home, Jay became the Continental Congress's secretary for foreign affairs — in effect, the nation's first secretary of state. In 1790, President George Washington named him the first chief justice of the United States Supreme Court. Four years later, the president sent him to London to negotiate a treaty with England that avoided the outbreak of another war.

Resigning as chief justice to become governor of New York, Jay pushed through a law for the gradual abolition of slavery. He had tried to insert a clause abolishing it when he wrote the state's constitution in 1777, but a majority of the legislature had rebuffed him. Jay never stopped insisting that slavery contradicted the meaning of the American Revolution.

By far the most famous of the many French volunteers from Catholic France was the nineteen-year-old

John Jay of New York was another descendant of French Protestants. A brilliant man, he was ambassador to Spain, helped negotiate the treaty of peace with England that ended the Revolutionary War, and was the first chief justice of the U.S. Supreme Court. As governor of New York, he won passage of a law that eliminated slavery.

Marquis de Lafayette. Born into nobility, this tall young Frenchman was one of the wealthiest men in Europe. He spent large amounts of his own money to help the cause. Congress made him a major general, and George Washington developed a deep affection for him.

At Valley Forge, Lafayette shared the bitter cold and awful food with his men, who called him "the soldier's friend." The marquis was awed by the soldiers' patience and devotion to the cause. He called it "a continual miracle."

In a stream of letters to his friends in France, the Marquis de Lafayette praised Washington's leadership. This testimony helped persuade **King Louis XVI** to become America's ally in the war. The alliance led to the climactic 1781 victory at Yorktown, Virginia, where a French fleet helped a combined French and American army trap a British army in the small tobacco port.

When the surrendered British marched out to lay down their guns, the American army was lined up on one side of the road and the French army on the other side. The British turned their faces toward the French and refused to acknowledge the Americans. An infuriated Lafayette ordered his band to strike

General Washington and the Marquis de Lafayette became close friends at the Valley Forge winter camp. Lafayette's letters to influential men in Paris praising Washington's leadership helped persuade the French to sign a treaty of alliance with the new republic.

up "Yankee Doodle." The shrilling fifes and beating drums jerked every British head in the Americans' direction. The king's men were forced to recognize their victorious former subjects.

The incident revealed how proud this young nobleman was of his ragged soldiers. Lafayette had become more American than French.

MANY JEWS VOLUNTEERED FOR WASHINGTON'S ARMY. NEW YORKER Isaac Franks was seventeen years old when he fought in the battle of Long Island in 1776. Wounded, he was taken prisoner by the British. Franks escaped and paddled across the Hudson River in a leaky boat to rejoin Washington's retreating army in New Jersey.

Benjamin Nones fought in two battles later in the war — Savannah, Georgia, and Charleston, South Carolina. His commanding officer wrote that the Jewish soldier's "behavior under fire in all the bloody battles we fought has been marked by the bravery and courage which a military man is expected to show."

One of the most important Jewish contributions to the American Revolution was made by a Polish-born immigrant named Haym Salomon. He not only raised

Outmaneuvered and outfought by the British in the Battle of Brooklyn, Americans fled across Gowanus Creek. A heroic attack by 250 Maryland soldiers, many of them Irish Americans, gave the fugitives time to escape.

Polacy! Kościuszko i Pułaski walczyli za wolność Polski i innych narodów! Idźmy w ich ślady! Hej na bój z wrogiem odwiecznym Polski i wolności!

POLES! KOSCIUSZKO AND PULASKI FOUGHT FOR THE LIBERTY OF POLAND AND OTHER NATIONS. FOLLOW THEIR EXAMPLE. ENLIST IN THE POLISH ARMY!

Thaddeus Kosciuszko tried to export the call to revolution to Poland in the 1780s and 1790s. Here he is in the center of a poster calling for recruits for the Polish army. But the Russians were too strong, and he was forced to abandon the struggle.

money for the federal government but also extended interest-free personal loans to many members of Congress, including **James Madison**. The young Virginian, who became the new country's fourth president, never forgot Salomon's generosity.

A PAIR OF POLISH OFFICERS, **COUNT CASIMIR PULASKI** AND **Colonel Thaddeus Kosciuszko**, won enduring fame in America's struggle for liberty. Count Pulaski led a legion, a force of cavalry and infantry, that fought courageously in several battles. About a dozen Polish volunteers were in the ranks. Pulaski died of wounds after leading a charge against British fortifications at Savannah, in 1779.

Colonel Kosciuszko was an engineer who designed and built crucial American defenses for the battle of Saratoga in 1777. "Kos," as his fellow officers called him, created redoubts so strong, the British hesitated to attack them. This gave the Americans the confidence to take the offensive in the battle and force the invaders to surrender. Later, Kosciuszko designed the defenses for West Point, the New York fortress that enabled the Americans to control the vital Hudson River during the closing years of the war.

SWISS IMMIGRANTS, WHO HAD A CENTURIES-OLD TRADITION OF LIBERTY, WERE FIRM supporters of independence in their new homeland. When the British, fearing an armed rebellion, refused to allow the colonists to import any more gunpowder, **Henry Wisner** established a powder mill in Goshen, New York. As a member of the Continental Congress, he pushed for the adoption of the Declaration of Independence and might well have been among its signers. By July 1776, however, he was back in Goshen supervising the production of ammunition for the American army.

THE CONTINENTAL ARMY'S OFFICER CORPS INCLUDED MANY DUTCH LEADERS. One of the most courageous was **Colonel Theunis Dey**, a descendant of a soldier who helped found the Dutch colony of New Netherlands in 1624. Colonel Dey commanded the rear guard during the American retreat across New Jersey in November 1776. Washington had lost most of his army in clashes with the

When six thousand British and German soldiers invaded New Jersey north of Fort Lee in November 1776, Washington was forced to retreat to Pennsylvania. The Americans had lost most of their army in the fighting around New York.

British around New York, and the British were in ferocious pursuit of the few men still willing to serve. Washington's choice of Colonel Dey was a tribute to the Dutchman's fighting spirit. He kept the pursuers at bay until the Americans reached safety on the west bank of the Delaware River.

THE WAR RAGED ON THE WESTERN FRONTIER AS WELL AS ON THE ATLANTIC coast. There, a seldom-recognized leader was Italian-born Joseph Maria

Francesco Vigo, who played a crucial role in the 1779 capture of the British fort at Vincennes, in what is now Indiana. Vigo guided the American expedition under the command of **General George Rogers Clark** across 240 miles of unmapped winter wilderness and also put up much of the money for their food, equipment, and ammunition. Together, Vigo and Clark won a large chunk of the territory that comprises the current states of Ohio, Indiana, Illinois, Michigan, and Wisconsin.

BY THE TIME THE REVOLUTIONARY WAR ENDED, LEADERS FROM MANY ETHNIC GROUPS had become famous in the new nation. **J. Hector St. Jean de Crevecoeur**, a Frenchman who lived on a farm in Orange County, New York, noted that "here individuals of all nations are melted into a new race of men." As proof of his statement, Crevecoeur cited a couple whose four sons were married to women of four different nationalities.

The leaders of the United States took special pride in the new nation's diversity. In December 1783, George Washington told a group of recent arrivals from Ireland, "The bosom of America is open to receive not only the opulent and respectable stranger but the oppressed and persecuted of all nations and religions. . . ."

Bernardo
DE GALVEZ

Bernardo de Galvez was only thirty years old when he became the governor of Louisiana. He helped the Americans with secret aid. When Spain joined the war against England in 1779, Galvez raised an army and won numerous victories. His army included many free blacks from New Orleans.

Although there were few if any Spaniards in the English colonies in 1775, they too played a role in the eventual American victory, thanks to thirty-year-old **Bernardo de Galvez**. When he became governor of Louisiana on January 1, 1777, the colony was a neglected backwater of the Spanish empire. The mostly French inhabitants had disliked the haughty aloofness of previous Spanish governors. (The colony was founded by France and given to Spain in 1762.) Galvez's personal charm and political ability changed everyone's attitude. He married a Frenchwoman and mingled freely with the people of New Orleans.

Galvez soon became a supporter of the American Revolution. He loaned thousands of dollars to **Oliver Pollock**, the Irish-born American representative in New Orleans. The money enabled Pollock to ship tons of ammunition and supplies up the Mississippi and Ohio rivers to Pittsburgh, Pennsylvania, to help the Americans fighting in the West.

When France persuaded Spain to enter the war in 1779, Galvez became a dynamic general. He captured British forts at Baton Rouge, Louisiana, and Natchez, Mississippi, and took more than one thousand prisoners. In the next two years, he captured

The capture of Pensacola, part of British-held Florida, was the most important victory won by Governor Bernardo de Galvez. In this picture, a British powder magazine inside the city explodes, enabling Galvez and his troops to attack and force the British to surrender.

British-held Mobile, Alabama, and Pensacola, Florida. The British had to commit thousands of men and numerous ships to these little-known clashes. They badly needed these soldiers and sailors to fight the Americans.

Whenever George Washington learned of a Galvez victory, he announced it to his troops and they celebrated. This gifted young Spaniard was the right man in the right place at the right time — for the United States of America.

CHAPTER TWO

REVOLUTION IN BLACK

African Americans participated in the American Revolution from its very first day. For a long time, they received no credit for their courage and enthusiasm for liberty.

The minutemen who fought at Lexington and Concord on April 19, 1775, included at least nine black soldiers. One, **Peter Salem**, served in a company from the town of Framingham, Massachusetts. His owner had given him his freedom so he could enlist. Another minuteman, **Pomp Blackman**, later became a regular in the Continental army. Yet another, **Prince Estabrook of Lexington**, was among the

Crispus Attucks, an African American seaman, was one of the leaders in an angry protest against a British decision to garrison troops in Boston. He and four other men were killed on March 5, 1770, in a clash soon known as the Boston Massacre. Attucks is visible at the center of this picture.

Peter Salem **was one of the many outstanding black fighters at the battle of Bunker Hill. Here, Peter Salem helps** Thomas Grosvenor **conduct a fighting retreat when the British finally overran the American fort.**

ninety American casualties on that historic day.

Two months later, American and British troops fought their first major battle at Bunker Hill. Once again, there were black men in the ranks, including former slave Peter Salem. Among the heroes at Bunker Hill was Salem Poor, a free black man from Groton, Connecticut. Fourteen officers who had fought in the battle submitted a petition to the Massachusetts legislature praising Poor. "In the person of this said Negro, centers a brave and gallant fellow," they declared.

When the Continental army was organized in July 1775, there was much discussion about recruiting black men. Although it was clear that Northern black men like Salem Poor made good soldiers, Southerners balked at arming their slaves. In many parts of the South, slaves greatly outnumbered whites. That made white leaders reluctant to give them weapons, lest they start a rebellion of their own.

Some months after George Washington became commander in chief of the Continental army, he met with his generals to consider including black men in the army. The majority voted to exclude all black men, both free and slave. When the decision was affirmed by the Continental Congress, Washington informed his black troops that when their terms of service expired on December 31, 1775, they would not be allowed to reenlist.

Soon after, a group of African American soldiers appeared at Washington's headquarters in Cambridge to protest the new policy. Sympathizing with their position, the general prevailed upon Congress to reverse its decision and allow free black men to reenlist. No new black men would be accepted, however, and slaves would continue to be excluded.

As the war continued, this policy was abandoned. In 1777, the Continental Congress, at Washington's request, required soldiers to enlist for three years. Each state was assigned a quota. The states ordered each town to provide a certain number of men. White men who were unwilling to commit to a three-year enlistment often hired black men to serve in their places. Soon more than 10 percent of the soldiers in the Continental army were black.

There were Irish, German, Dutch, and African American soldiers in the ranks when George Washington crossed the Delaware River on Christmas night 1776 to win a crucial victory at Trenton, New Jersey.

Typical of these men was **Oliver Cromwell** of New Jersey, who crossed the Delaware River with George Washington on Christmas night, 1776, to help win a crucial victory over the enemy garrison in Trenton. **Aaron Carter** of Connecticut enlisted in 1777 as a substitute for a white man. So did Aaron's four brothers, **Jacob**, **Asher**, **Edward**, and **Esau**. So many Connecticut black men joined the army

REVOLUTION IN BLACK

in exchange for their freedom that they formed an entire company in one regiment.

In 1778, the Rhode Island General Assembly passed a law allowing General James Varnum to recruit a regiment of African Americans. The Assembly guaranteed that when the war was over, they would be "absolutely free." Some two hundred black men signed up, and the First Rhode Island Regiment was formed.

A few months later, General John Sullivan arrived in Rhode Island with a plan to attack and destroy the British army in Newport. The French, who had recently become America's allies in the war, were sending a fleet of warships to help him. The First Rhode Island Regiment was part of Sullivan's army.

Sullivan and the French admiral decided the Americans would land on the north end of Aquidneck Island, where Newport is situated. The French would land troops on the west side of the island, and the two armies would join and assault the British forces.

Sullivan crossed Narragansett Bay and landed on Aquidneck with ten thousand troops. While they were marching south, the British fleet appeared off Newport. The French admiral sailed out to fight them without informing General Sullivan of the change in plans. Suddenly, a tremendous storm erupted. The British fleet withdrew south to New York, and the battered French ships sought refuge north in Boston,

"If they had given way, all would have been lost."

leaving Sullivan's army isolated on Aquidneck Island. "To evacuate is death," groaned one American general. "To stay is ruin."

Several regiments of part-time American soldiers, known as militia, gave up and went home. Left with only half of his original army, Sullivan retreated to the north end of Aquidneck. The British army followed him, confident that they could mount a successful attack as the Americans struggled to get their men and equipment aboard their boats to escape to the mainland.

General Sullivan decided to show the French and the British that Americans had not lost their fighting spirit. He detached the First Rhode Island and several other regiments, and ordered them to keep the enemy at bay so the rest of his army could escape.

It was the black regiment's first time in battle. The British general ordered veteran German regiments in his army to attack them. Offshore, four men-of-war pounded the Americans with heavy guns. The First Rhode Island stood its ground. Three times the Germans charged with leveled bayonets; three times the black soldiers drove them back in confusion. "If they had given way," a white soldier who was in the battle wrote later, "all would have been lost."

Rhode Island was the first American state to raise an entire regiment of black soldiers. In this painting, titled *Desperate Valor*, these new troops distinguish themselves in their first battle near Newport in 1778. Three times they beat off attacks by veteran German troops fighting for the British.

General Sullivan was able to report to George Washington that he had evacuated all his supplies and baggage. Most important, "not a man was left behind." From that day, the First Rhode Island was considered one of the best regiments in the American army. "They were brave hardy troops," wrote the same white soldier.

In 1779, "the biggest, the tallest, the most imposing Negress" in the state of Georgia, a woman known only as **Mammy Kate**, rescued her master from his British captors. The man, **Stephen Heard**, had been taken prisoner because of his sympathies with the patriots and was being held at a fort in Augusta. There was every reason to believe the British planned to execute him. Mammy Kate rode fifty miles on horseback from the Heard plantation to the fort. Hiding the horse a mile or two away, she approached the fort on foot, carrying a large clothes basket. She told the sentry on duty that she was a washerwoman. Did any of the officers want their laundry done?

Almost all the officers did, so Mammy Kate quickly built up a thriving business. Once she had become a regular visitor to the fort, she asked the British if their American prisoner might like to have his laundry done, too. Again the answer was yes.

From then on, Mammy Kate was admitted to Stephen Heard's prison cell twice a week. She left with a huge stack of dirty laundry in her basket and returned a few days later with a pile of freshly washed clothes.

One evening, as it was getting dark, Mammy Kate left the prison as usual with her basket balanced on her head. Instead of dirty laundry, however, the slightly built Stephen Heard was huddled inside. Mammy Kate and her master were soon riding off to safety.

Stephen Heard, who later became governor of Georgia, was so grateful to Mammy Kate that he freed her and gave her a plot of land and a house. Mammy Kate continued to work for the Heard family until her death.

In 1781, the Marquis de Lafayette arrived in Williamsburg, Virginia, with a small American army to oppose a British invasion of the state. The enemy army

Stephen Heard was one of the leaders of the Revolution in Georgia. Here he rides to battle on his swift horse, Silverheels. Georgia was bitterly divided between loyalists and rebels.

The Marquis de Lafayette persuaded the Virginians to make James Armistead a free man for his courageous service as a spy.

heavily outnumbered Lafayette's men. A local patriot, **William Armistead**, offered the Frenchman one of his slaves to serve as his valet. The slave, **Jim**, was a daring and resourceful young man who soon volunteered to become a spy.

Pretending to be a runaway, Jim walked into the British camp at Portsmouth, Virginia, and vastly exaggerated the strength of Lafayette's army, making the British hesitate to attack him. The British were so impressed that they hired Jim to spy on Lafayette! The Marquis de Lafayette fed him more lies about the whereabouts of Washington's army, which was marching to Virginia. Jim's role as a double agent helped to trap the British when they retreated to Yorktown.

After the war, Lafayette procured Jim's freedom. Forty-three years later, in 1824, Lafayette returned to America for a triumphant tour on the eve of the fiftieth anniversary of the Declaration of Independence. As the French hero rode through Richmond, Virginia, Jim stepped out of the crowd and shook his hand. Lafayette was pleased to discover that Jim had adopted his surname and was now called James Lafayette.

Except for a few Quakers, not many people criticized slavery before the Revolution. The few who spoke out were usually dismissed as oddballs. However, fighting a war that proclaimed all men were created equal and were entitled to life, liberty, and the pursuit of happiness forced many Americans to think hard about slavery.

One of them was Benjamin Franklin. Toward the end of his long life, he accepted the presidency of the Society for the Abolition of Slavery. Franklin wrote a petition to Congress urging the legislators to begin a program of "gradual manumission" that would free all of America's slaves over the course of two or three decades.

Within twenty years of the end of the Revolution, all the Northern states had eliminated slavery through gradual manumission laws. Even in the Southern states, a surprising number of slave owners freed their slaves. By the time the Civil War began in 1860, there were five hundred thousand free black people in America. Another four million remained slaves.

What does all this mean? **Christopher Brown**, a talented young black historian, summed it up admirably when he called the Revolution a "world-transforming event" in the history of slavery. For the first time in two thousand years, the slave system was challenged. In less than a century, it was dead.

James FORTEN

At the age of fourteen, **James Forten** became one of the many African Americans who served in America's Revolutionary navy. Born free in Philadelphia, Pennsylvania, he went to sea as a powder boy aboard the privateer *Royal Louis*.

On her second voyage, the *Royal Louis* encountered three British warships and was forced to surrender. The captain of one of the British ships offered to take Forten to England and pay for his education — if he would give up his allegiance to the United States.

"No," Forten said. "I was captured fighting for my country. I will never be a traitor to her interests."

Forten was sent to the British prison ship *Jersey* in New York harbor. The food was abominable, and the air was thick with sickening odors and disease. Forten's hair fell out, and he was reduced to a skeleton by the time the war ended and he was released.

Returning to Philadelphia, Forten became an apprentice to a sailmaker. He learned the

"I was captured fighting for my country.

trade so well that he was promoted to foreman; when the owner retired, he left the business to Forten. He was soon a wealthy man.

Forten remained deeply troubled by the hundreds of thousands of African Americans who remained slaves. Well-intentioned white people bought land in Africa and founded the nation of Liberia. They offered freedom to African Americans if they agreed to settle there. The white people hoped that eventually most other African Americans would join them and slavery in the United States would be peacefully eliminated.

The leaders of the Liberian experiment proposed to make James Forten the president of this new nation. Forten refused the honor. He said he would rather remain "a sailmaker in Philadelphia than enjoy the highest offices" of Liberia. Once and for all, the United States had to understand that black people were Americans, too. "Here we were born, here we will live, here we will die," Forten said.

When James Forten died in 1842, four thousand people attended his funeral. Half were black, half were white. "He was a model," one man wrote, "not only for his own race, but for all men."

Philadelphian James Forten.

I will never be a traitor to her interests."

CHAPTER THREE

WARRIORS FOR THE REPUBLIC

In mid-May 1778, startling news swept through the Continental army at Valley Forge. There were Indians in the camp! They were not there to fight Americans but to join the American side. Off-duty soldiers rushed to get a look at this unusual sight.

In a solid column, forty-nine tall, muscular members of the **Oneida Nation** strode past the one thousand huts where the Americans had endured semistarvation and freezing temperatures during the previous winter. The Indians were accompanied by a Frenchman, **Chevalier Anne-Louis de Tousard**, a friend of the

Indians from several small tribes in New England and the South had volunteered to fight for the Americans early in the war. This may have given the Marquis de Lafayette, seen here with George Washington, the idea to invite the Oneida Nation to send a forty-nine-man fighting force in May 1778.

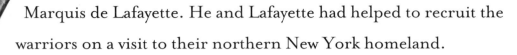

Marquis de Lafayette. He and Lafayette had helped to recruit the warriors on a visit to their northern New York homeland.

Down the road the warriors went to General Washington's headquarters. There, the commander in chief greeted them with great solemnity. He asked Tousard, who spoke their language, to tell the warriors the United States welcomed and appreciated their help in the struggle for liberty.

Two of General Washington's staff officers escorted the Oneida to the artillery park, about a mile away. As they arrived, the commander of the artillery, General Henry Knox, ordered a thirteen-gun salute to the army's new allies.

The army's commissaries, the officers in charge of issuing food, treated the newcomers to a feast of well-cooked beef and pork and fish. On their two-hundred-mile journey from northern New York, they had lived on a few handfuls of parched corn each day.

On May 17, General Washington gave the Oneida an important assignment. He wanted them to help 2,200 Americans, led by the Marquis

For close-quarter combat, Indians favored the tomahawk *(left)* and the ballheaded club *(right)*. They were also good shots with the rifle and musket.

de Lafayette, keep a close watch on the British army that was occupying Philadelphia. There were rumors that the British might retreat to New York. If they tried this, Lafayette had orders to attack their rear guard as they crossed the Delaware River.

The Americans camped at Barren Hill, Pennsylvania, about twelve miles from Philadelphia. The Oneida warriors joined fifty veteran riflemen from the Virginia frontier and roamed the surrounding roads and woods to make sure the British did not make a surprise attack on Lafayette's men.

In Philadelphia, a deserter from Lafayette's army told the British where Lafayette was camped and how many men he had. The British decided to attack the Americans with nine thousand men — almost every soldier in their army.

They wanted to capture Lafayette and take him back to London as a prisoner. France's **King Louis XVI** had just signed an alliance with the Americans, and capturing the marquis would make the king — and General Washington — look foolish.

As dawn was breaking on May 20, the Oneida and the American riflemen heard an ominous sound on the road: the tramp of marching feet. Looming up in the gray light were two or three hundred British cavalry and thousands of foot soldiers. The Americans and the Oneida immediately opened fire, throwing the

column into confusion. The British fired back, and for a few minutes bullets whizzed among the trees.

The British, realizing they were being attacked by barely a hundred men, ordered a cavalry charge to scatter them. A troop of saber-wielding dragoons thundered toward the Americans and Oneida, roaring death and destruction. The Oneida responded with their own special brand of defiance. As one voice, they released a tremendous war whoop.

Neither the British horses nor the men in the saddles had ever heard anything like it. Horses bolted and dragoons leaped to the ground, running for their lives. It took the British another ten minutes to reorganize and order the infantry to advance with fixed bayonets. The scouts and the Oneida fell back, firing steadily.

When they reached Barren Hill, the skirmishers found Lafayette's army retreating. They had been alerted by the gunfire and realized that they were being attacked by an overwhelming force. The Oneida and the scouts formed a rear guard and fought off British attacks as Lafayette's army double-timed it to a nearby ford across the Schuylkill River.

At the ford, the Oneida were again attacked by cavalrymen, who knocked

The British persuaded thousands of Indians to fight on their side in the war. Here, British General John Burgoyne addresses warriors from several nations in July 1777, as he began his invasion of northern New York.

Tousard off his horse and killed several other Frenchmen who had accompanied the expedition. At the risk of their lives, two Oneida braves seized the dazed Tousard and dragged him across the river. On the opposite bank, the Americans blasted bullets at the horsemen, forcing them to retreat.

From Valley Forge came the boom of alarm guns. General Washington and the rest of the American army were marching to help Lafayette and his men. The frustrated British retreated to Philadelphia.

George Washington was deeply impressed by the courage of the Oneida and their fighting abilities. The following year, at his recommendation, one of the Oneida Nation's leading warriors, **Lewis Atayataghronghta**, was given a commission as a lieutenant colonel in the American army. Seven other Oneida and two members of the **Tuscarora Nation**, who had also joined the war, were commissioned as American lieutenants and captains. For the rest of the war, these Indian officers and their followers fought the British and their Indian allies in northern New York.

The Oneida and Tuscarora were not the only Indian peoples to fight on the American side. Early in the war, the **Stockbridge Indians** of Massachusetts formed a company of warriors and volunteered their services to the Americans. Another small tribe, the **Mashpee** of Cape Cod, also sent volunteers. So did the **Catawba** of the western Carolinas. But none of these matched the Oneida Nation's contribution. An estimated three hundred Oneida warriors fought for the United States.

The Oneida paid a harsh price for their devotion to the American cause. In the closing years of the war, they were attacked by the **Mohawk** and other tribes loyal to the British. They burned Oneida villages and killed many of their men and women. Yet, the Oneida Nation remained loyal to the Americans. They had pledged their honor to fight for them, and they continued to do so until the end of the war.

When peace came in 1783, the grateful Americans awarded Lewis Atayataghronghta and his officers and men grants of land for their courage and devotion during the long struggle for freedom from England.

This is the text of a speech given in 1780 by two **Oneida** chiefs desperately asking their American allies for help. The other nations of the Iroquois Confederacy were threatening to annihilate the Oneida for siding with the Americans. The chiefs want the Americans to provide a safe place for their women and children.

Divided LOYALTIES

The 200,000 American Indians living east of the Mississippi were divided into eighty-five different nations or tribes. Some, like the **Iroquois**, were confederacies, or leagues of several tribes. (The Oneida were part of the Iroquois confederacy.) The British not only gave them presents of money and weapons, but they also promised to defeat the Americans and help the Indians preserve their tribal lands from white settlers.

Most of the **Cherokee** and Iroquois took arms against the Americans. In the West, the **Shawnee** and other tribes backed the British for the same reason. The results were disastrous for all of them.

The Indians did not realize there were 2.1 million white people in America. That meant the Indians could win victories against isolated frontier settlements but they could not defeat the overwhelming forces the Americans mustered in response to these attacks. In 1776, the states of Georgia, South Carolina, North Carolina, and Virginia sent eight thousand men against the

In retaliation for Indian raids on isolated settlements in northern New York and Pennsylvania, General Washington ordered Major General John Sullivan of New Hampshire and a four-thousand-man army to invade the Iroquois region of New York. The Americans burned villages and destroyed crops, forcing the Indians to flee to Canada.

Warfare between Indians and white settlers continued to rage in northern New York until the end of the Revolution. Here, a Seneca warrior attacks a Cherry Valley family in 1778. When the British signed a peace treaty and declared that the war was over, the Indians felt betrayed by their former allies.

Cherokee. They routed their warriors, burned their villages, and forced them to remain peaceful for the rest of the war.

In 1777, the Iroquois, led by a chief named **Joseph Brant**, burned more than one thousand homes in a raid on the Wyoming Valley in Pennsylvania. They devastated other settlements in northern New York, such as Cherry Valley. In 1779, a four-thousand-man army led by Major General John Sullivan invaded the Iroquois' homeland in northwestern New York. The Iroquois fled to Canada, abandoning their villages to destruction.

In the West, the Shawnee captured two American forts and terrorized frontier settlements. General George Rogers Clark led one thousand riflemen into their homeland and burned their "mother town" of Chillicothe, Ohio.

In spite of these defeats, some Indians vowed to keep fighting. They were stunned when the British quit the war and granted America independence. The Americans considered the hostile Indian nations conquered enemies and tried to seize their land. Some Indians resisted, and there was more bloodshed. Finally, Congress decided to negotiate with the Indians as separate nations worthy of respect. This policy reduced the bloodshed, but many tensions remained in the relationship between white Americans and American Indians.

At the invitation of the Continental Congress, a delegation from the Iroquois League visited Philadelphia and was welcomed in May 1776 with great ceremony. The Iroquois pledged they would remain neutral in the war. The visit demonstrated how hard the Americans tried to maintain friendly relations with the Indians.

WARRIORS FOR THE REPUBLIC

CHAPTER FOUR

WOMEN AT WAR

Although the American Revolution was fought mostly by men, colonial women did not shirk from waging a few battles of their own. The year before Lexington and Concord, fifty-one women in Edenton, North Carolina, backed a boycott on all British-made products. They signed a statement that declared they could not be indifferent to a political quarrel that affected the peace and happiness of their country. The boycott was an attempt to force the British to negotiate a political settlement rather than resort to war.

Present-day readers may not realize how unusual it once was for women to

This picture portrays "Molly Pitcher" at the 1778 battle of Monmouth. Her real name was Mary Ludwig Hays. When her artillerist husband was wounded during the battle, she supposedly took his place in his gun crew. Several other women were also called Molly Pitcher because they carried water to soldiers during a battle.

become involved in politics. **Esther Edwards Burr**, mother of the future senator and vice president, Aaron Burr, told a friend: "The men say that women have no business to concern themselves about 'em [politics] but trust to those that know better." The furor over the struggle for liberty was so intense that women soon ignored this supposed principle. **Sarah Franklin** told her father, Benjamin Franklin: "Nothing else is talked of." As **Annis Boudinot Stockton**, wife of a member of the Continental Congress, put it: "Tho a female, I was born a patriot and can't help it if I would."

When the war broke out, many women shifted to direct action. When their husbands joined the Continental army, women often went with them. Washington issued them daily rations but insisted they had to earn their keep. Many women became laundresses, a very important job. Without clean clothes, soldiers developed skin diseases. Others worked as cooks. Only a few became nurses. To prevent disease from spreading, hospitals were usually many miles from the army's camps.

Other women served as spies inside British-occupied New York and Philadelphia. **Lydia Darragh**, who was an undertaker as well as a nurse and midwife, lived in a house near the Philadelphia headquarters of the British commander in chief, **Sir William Howe**. One of Howe's officers ordered her to set aside a room as a council chamber for the British general's staff.

It so happened that Mrs. Darragh's bedroom was on the floor above the meeting room. One night, she overheard the officers plotting a surprise attack on the American camp at Whitemarsh, a few miles outside the city.

During the Revolution, American women often gathered to discuss the war and plan campaigns to raise money to buy clothes for General Washington's soldiers. Here, women participate in a "quilting bee" — sewing a warm quilt to give to the army and exchanging news about the war.

The next day, she wangled a pass from Howe's headquarters, explaining that she needed to buy some flour at a mill in a nearby village. She left Philadelphia carrying an empty flour sack in her hand, which seemed to confirm her story.

Once she got past the British lines, however, Darragh began

Philadelphian Lydia
Darragh was one
of America's most
successful female spies.
Here, she is questioned
by a suspicious British
officer.

walking toward Whitemarsh. After a few miles, she encountered an American officer and told him what she had overheard. When Howe's troops marched to Whitemarsh early the next morning, the Americans were ready for them. After a few days of ineffectual skirmishes, the discouraged British headed back to Philadelphia.

Not long after that encounter, Washington moved his army to Valley Forge. Lydia Darragh's oldest son, Charles, a lieutenant in a Pennsylvania brigade, went with him. Mrs. Darragh regularly sent letters to Charles, using her fourteen-year-old son, John, as a messenger.

The notes were bland enough. If a British sentry read them, he would have no reason to think there was anything suspicious about them. The sentries never discovered that John was carrying far more important messages stuffed inside the large buttons on his coat. Thanks to Lydia Darragh, George Washington had ample information about the British forces in Philadelphia.

Some women saw combat. Among the most daring was **Deborah Sampson**, an unusually strong and adventurous young woman who enlisted in the Fourth Massachusetts Regiment under the name of Robert Shurtleff. She took part in several engagements and was wounded in a skirmish near Tarrytown, New York.

Sampson's identity was concealed until the war was almost over. It was discovered only because she was taken ill with a fever and had to be hospitalized. Deborah Sampson, aka Robert Shurtleff, was discharged from the army by General Henry Knox at West Point on October 25, 1783.

Twenty-five-year-old **Margaret Cochran Corbin** took her husband's place at his cannon after he was killed in the battle of Fort Washington, New York, in 1776. Wounded three times, Margaret Corbin became the first woman to receive a military pension from Congress.

At the 1778 battle of Monmouth, a woman who has never been identified was close enough to the fighting to see her husband struck down by a British bullet. She raced to his side, seized his gun, and in the words of an eyewitness, "like a Spartan

Deborah Sampson of Massachusetts enlisted in Washington's army as a man and served for more than a year. After the war she had a successful career as a lecturer, describing her adventures. Eventually she married and had three children.

heroine [began] discharging the piece with as much regularity as any soldier present."

Other women exhibited daring and courage off the battlefield. In 1780, the struggle between loyalists and rebel Americans in Georgia was dubbed "the war of extermination." Six-foot-tall **Nancy Hart** lived in the midst of this terror with her eight children. Her husband was fighting on the side of liberty, and she knew she could expect little kindness from the enemy.

One night, five loyalists invaded Nancy's cabin. They called her unpleasant names and demanded dinner. Nancy was polite, humble, and almost contrite. She gave them all the food and liquor they could possibly want. She urged them to relax and lay aside their guns. She soon had the guns stacked in the corner and her guests on their way to getting drunk.

Summoning one of her daughters, Nancy ordered her to fetch some fresh water. At the door, she whispered to the girl that she should run as fast as her legs could carry her to the nearest American outpost and bring help. When ten or fifteen minutes elapsed with no sign of the girl or the water, one of the enemy became suspicious.

"Where did you send that brat?" he roared, staggering to his feet.

Nancy grabbed four of the guns and heaved them out the window. She kept one, which she aimed at the man's chest. "I can shoot this thing," she said. "Maybe you better sit down."

The man sat down, and no one moved until American soldiers showed up and took the humiliated loyalists prisoner. Nancy lived to the age of ninety. In 1853, the State of Georgia named a county after her.

Many women served the patriots in more traditional ways. During the Valley Forge winter of 1777–1778, **Mary Frazier** of Chester County, Pennsylvania, made numerous trips through the countryside, knocking on doors and collecting blankets, coats, and socks for the half-naked soldiers. She sat up countless nights darning and patching worn clothes and then packed them in her wagon for the journey to the winter camp.

In May 1777, twenty women in Poughkeepsie, New York, led Continental soldiers to the home of **Peter Mesier**, a merchant who was suspected of hoarding tea. Mesier's wife offered to sell them the hidden tea at four dollars a pound. The women brushed her aside and marched into the house. Armed with scales, they proceeded to weigh as much tea as they could carry away and paid for it at a far lower price than Mesier had been charging.

In Boston, in 1778, more than one hundred women took even more vigorous action against a greedy merchant who was suspected of hoarding coffee. When he refused to yield the keys to his warehouse, one of the women seized him by the neck. He quickly handed over the keys, and the women invaded the building. They retreated only after they had taken every sack of coffee they could lay their hands on.

A delighted **Abigail Adams** reported this incident in a letter to her husband, John, who was on a diplomatic mission in Europe. Abigail gleefully added that "a large concourse of men stood amazed silent spectators."

In 1776, Abigail Adams had urged her husband to "remember the ladies" in the new government that he and his fellow members of the Continental Congress were putting together. Although John Adams brushed her off with a few teasing remarks, the exchange was important, no matter how meager the immediate results. The letter

"born for liberty. . ."

symbolized the transformation that the Revolution made in American women's consciousness. Instead of accepting their male-imposed role as humble helpmates, they began to speak and act independently.

A good example is a 1779 campaign launched by the women of Philadelphia to raise money for Washington's soldiers. They began the drive with a broadside entitled "The Sentiments of an American Woman."

The statement declared that American women were "born for liberty" and disdained to "bear the irons of a tyrannic government." The women went on to declare that opinion and manners forbade them to march to glory by the same paths as men, but they were determined to be at least equal, and perhaps stronger, in their loyalty to the American republic.

They proved these words by working hard at their fund-raising, collecting more than 300,000 dollars.

Abigail Adams, wife of Congressman John Adams, was one of the most outspoken American women of the Revolution. She urged John to "remember the ladies" in the new government the men were creating. Abigail declared that women had rights and that it was time men respected them.

When **Esther Reed**, who headed the committee, informed George Washington of this impressive sum, he suggested that the women deposit it in the new Bank of North America, where it would be united with the money of "the gentlemen" who were also trying to help the army.

Mrs. Reed coolly rejected this idea. She said they wanted to give the soldiers a gift that came directly from the women to the men. Further negotiations resulted in a decision to buy enough linen to make shirts for the soldiers.

All things considered, the women clearly won this polite clash with the general. They gave the soldiers something that was unmistakably from the women of Philadelphia.

A generation later, in the 1830s, women began sending petitions to Congress to abolish slavery. Former president **John Quincy Adams**, Abigail Adams's son, used the example of the Philadelphia broadside to defend women's rights to participate in the political world. He insisted that women could be patriots and that they had "political rights," even if these rights were not formally endorsed by the Constitution. It took almost a hundred years, but the rest of the country eventually agreed with him. In 1920, the Nineteenth Amendment gave women the right to vote.

American women often took strenuous action to defy the British. In this picture, Mrs. Philip Schuyler of Albany, New York, sets fire to her family's cornfields to prevent them from being harvested by an invading British army in 1777.

Agent 13

Few women contributed more to the American cause than the beautiful New Yorker known to the American secret service as **Agent 13**. She became a member of a group of American spies known as the "Culper ring." Based partly on Long Island, they collected information through **Robert Townsend**, one of their agents who pretended to be loyal to the king and lived in British-occupied New York.

Townsend depended on Agent 13 for much of his information. She was a member of the wealthy upper class who mingled with British officers in the occupied city. At dinner parties and balls, she listened to the officers as they talked about the army's plans, and she passed on the information to Townsend, who smuggled it out to Long Island. From there, another member of the ring smuggled it across Long Island Sound to Connecticut, where it was rushed to General Washington.

Agent 13's greatest coup was the discovery that the British planned to attack and destroy the small French army that had arrived in Newport, Rhode Island, to fight beside the Americans in 1780. A victory would have knocked France out of the war. When General Washington heard about this plan, he made sure the British soon discovered an American plan to assault New York. The plan existed only in Washington's imagination, but the British abandoned their attack on the French.

The British prison ship *Jersey* was anchored off the Brooklyn shore. The food was abominable and disease was rampant. An estimated eleven thousand Americans died aboard the *Jersey* and other prison ships.

Realizing their plan had been betrayed, the infuriated British launched an investigation that led them to Agent 13. She was arrested and put aboard a disease-ridden prison ship in New York harbor. There she soon died and was buried in an unmarked grave. No one has ever learned her name. Robert Townsend, the spy who knew her (and may have loved her), went to his grave without revealing it.

CHAPTER FIVE

YOUNG PEOPLE AT WAR

In 1775, almost all Americans could read. This enabled young people to follow the political arguments that preceded the shooting war. Many were enthusiastic about independence, even though they were too young to vote or fight.

Few youngsters were a better example of this enthusiasm than fourteen-year-old **Joseph Plumb Martin** of Connecticut. On April 21, 1775, he was plowing a field about a half mile from his home when the church bells began to ring. He rushed to find out "what the commotion was" and discovered that war had begun in Massachusetts. All the "male kind of the people" were volunteering to march to

Sixteen-year-old Sybil Ludington became a female Paul Revere when she rode through the night for five hours to turn out American militiamen to fight a British raid on Danbury, Connecticut, in 1777.

The Spirit of 1776 is one of the most famous paintings of the Revolution. Not many people notice that the drummer is very young. Many drummers (and fifers) in Washington's army were boys.

Boston to fight the British. Watching, Martin wished he were old enough to join them.

A year later, Martin persuaded his grandparents, with whom he lived, to let him join the army. According to the law, a man had to be seventeen to join up, but recruiters seldom asked questions about a volunteer's age. Martin stayed in the army until America won its independence, eight years later. In his old age, he wrote a fascinating book describing his "adventures, dangers, and sufferings" as a Revolutionary soldier.

Twelve-year-old **Ebenezer Fox** came from a poor family in Roxbury, Massachusetts. His parents had "bound him out" to work on a neighbor's farm. He decided the Revolutionary excitement gave him a perfect excuse to run away and "set up a government of my own." He and a friend headed for Providence,

Rhode Island, where they were hired as sailors on an American ship.

These young people felt the spirit of liberty sweeping the country. Typical of them was sixteen-year-old **William Diamond**, who signed up as drummer boy in the Lexington, Massachusetts, militia company. On April 19, 1775, Diamond beat "to arms" on his brightly painted drum. That sound brought seventy militiamen to confront approaching British regulars. Young Diamond was in the ranks when the first shots of the war were fired.

Drummers were very important in the warfare of the Revolution. An officer's voice often could not be heard above the booming muskets and cannons. The various drumbeats gave the soldiers orders in camp, on the march, and in battle. The drummers were as exposed as the soldiers to the bullets that were flying from the enemy's guns. It took courage to be a drummer.

Other young men served as trumpeters in the cavalry. One of the most dramatic paintings of the Revolution tells the story of **Colonel William Washington** (a cousin of George Washington) dueling a British cavalry officer with sabers. When Colonel Washington's saber snapped, he was in imminent danger of death. From nowhere came his trumpeter, a young black slave about twelve years old,

whose name remains unknown. The boy fired a pistol, disabling the British officer's horse and saving Colonel Washington's life.

Young women were equally eager to serve their country. **Charity Clark** of New York told her British cousin that "heroines may not distinguish themselves at the head of an army." However, that did not mean women were indifferent to liberty's cause. Charity also told her cousin that she "felt Nationly" and was determined to help defend her country against Britain's "arbitrary power."

Young women soon proved they were ready to do extraordinary things. Sixteen-year-old **Sybil Ludington** lived in Fredericksburg, New York, only a few miles from Danbury, Connecticut. Her father was the colonel of the local militia regiment. Danbury's warehouses and barns were crammed with tons of food and ammunition for the American army. In April 1777, the British decided to attack them.

Landing near Fairfield, Connecticut, on Long Island Sound, a two-thousand-man strike force marched inland. The Americans were caught flat-footed. Scarcely a shot was fired at the column of redcoats as they tramped through the stunned countryside. By 3:00 P.M. on the day after they landed, they were in Danbury, burning the town.

At the close of the battle of Cowpens, a young African American trumpeter saved Colonel William Washington's life.

Captains of American privateers look for volunteers outside a recruiting office in New London, Connecticut. Many young boys served aboard these warships.

That evening, word of the disaster reached the Ludington household. Militiamen were being summoned from all points of the compass to trap the raiders before they escaped to their ships.

Colonel Ludington turned to Sybil and told her to spread the word among the members of his militia regiment to muster on the road to Danbury. She leaped on her horse and for the next five hours raced through the darkness, rapping on farmhouse doors with a stick, shouting the alarm. She covered more than forty miles before she returned home — a ride twice as long as Paul Revere's.

Colonel Ludington's regiment joined other Americans in vigorous pursuit of the British. Although most of the enemy reached their ships, dozens of men were lost in skirmishes along the way. They never attempted to march into the interior of Connecticut again.

On the frontier, marauding pro-British Indians seized **Jemima Boone**, the fourteen-year-old daughter of **Daniel Boone**, and two of her friends while they were canoeing on the Kentucky River. Knowing their fathers and several other men were on the way to rescue them, the feisty young women did everything possible to delay their captors.

They fell down and complained of foot and leg injuries. They said they were too exhausted to walk another yard. When the exasperated Indians stole a horse for them to ride, the young women refused to mount it. Boone and his men soon caught up with the harassed warriors and routed them with a blast of gunfire. The young women rode home unharmed.

For sheer daring, few women — or men — could match the courage of sixteen-year-old **Elizabeth Zane** of Virginia. She was the sister of **Ebenezer Zane**, who had led a group of pioneers west in search of new land and opportunity. (He became known as the founder of Wheeling, West Virginia.) In 1782, their small settlement was attacked by the British and their Indian allies.

In 1782, sixteen-year-old Elizabeth Zane risked Indian bullets to rush gunpowder to the defenders of Fort Henry in western Virginia.

The outnumbered citizens fled to nearby Fort Henry for safety.

For a while, Ebenezer Zane and the other men in the log fort held off the attackers. But the Americans' gunpowder supply began running low and they feared they might have to surrender. There was a keg of powder in the Zane house, about fifty yards from the fort. Several men volunteered to get it but Elizabeth insisted that she should go. The enemy would hesitate to shoot her because she was a woman.

Slipping out the fort's gate, Elizabeth coolly strolled to the Zane house as the puzzled British and Indians watched her without firing a shot. In the house, she wrapped the keg of powder in her apron and raced toward the fort. The startled enemy opened fire, but Elizabeth reached the gate unhurt. The fresh supply of powder enabled Ebenezer Zane and his men to hold out until reinforcements arrived and routed the attackers.

In 1781, Joseph Plumb Martin, who had enlisted at fifteen, was now twenty-one. He had the pleasure of witnessing the surrender of the British army at Yorktown, Virginia, that ended the war. As the British soldiers marched out to lay down their guns, a delighted Martin called it "a noble sight" because it promised "a speedy conclusion to the contest."

When the war began, Martin was a boy, and the United States of America was a haphazard collection of thirteen former colonies. Now Joseph Plumb Martin was a man — and a proud soldier who had proved his courage on a dozen battlefields. The United States was a united country, ready to take its place among the nations of the world.

Joseph COLLINS

When the Revolutionary War began in 1775, Joseph Collins of South Carolina was only eleven years old. Five years later, he was sixteen and the war had arrived on his doorstep. A British army invaded the state, captured the capital, Charleston, and surged into the countryside. Joseph's father and older brother joined the struggle against the king's men. At first, Joseph served as a "collector of news," reporting to the fighting Americans where the enemy was camping or marching.

The enemy also had collectors of news. They spied on Joseph's band of fighters and attacked when the Americans least expected it. Afterward, Joseph gazed at his dead and bleeding friends and thought: "If this be the fate of war, I would willingly be excused." However, he decided "the thing had gone too far. There was no safety in retreating." From one of the dead men he took a "good-looking rifle" and became a soldier.

In his first battle, at King's Mountain on October 7, 1780, Joseph Collins helped win a victory. The patriots defeated an army of loyalists, or Tories, as Collins called them. The aftermath was far more shocking than the results of the small battle he had witnessed earlier. The dead lay

At the battle of King's Mountain in 1780, many members of the American army were teenagers. Not a few came with their fathers from Tennessee to fight the loyalists who were entrenched on the mountain. The victory was a turning point in the struggle for control of the South.

"in heaps," while the wounded groaned everywhere. "The situation of the poor Tories seemed truly pitiable," Collins thought. Tears of compassion streamed down his face.

At Cowpens, South Carolina, on January 17, 1781, Collins helped win another important battle. However, he came very close to being killed with a bayonet by charging British infantry. "Now my hide is in the loft," he thought, as he fired his gun and retreated. Only later did he realize that the American general, **Daniel Morgan**, had let the British attack Collins and his fellow militiamen so he could counterattack with his regulars, who smashed the redcoats into surrender.

After each battle, Joseph set down in his diary exactly how many shots he fired; but he always said he had no idea whether he hit anyone. Although Joseph Collins was a patriot, he was also an honest man. He regretted the human cost of the war.

AFTERWORD

Without a doubt, the United States was created by men and women of many nationalities, races, and creeds. That is an important part of the reason why the Revolution's central ideas — liberty and equality — have had a profound impact not only on our country and its citizens, but on the whole world.

Some of the men and women of 1776 sensed the coming greatness of America. They saw that the Revolution was not simply a war for territory. It was a spiritual enterprise that would never end.

One of the finest testimonies to this sense of the Revolution's enduring power was written by Nathanael Ames, author of a popular almanac of 1776. He predicted that in an independent America "arts and sciences will change the Face of Nature" from the Appalachian Mountains to the "Western Ocean." He foresaw "treasures of gold and silver and mountains of iron ore" that would launch industries for "millions of hands" in great cities, creating prosperity that all Americans would share. Finally, Ames spoke directly to us, the Revolution's heirs.

"O! ye unborn inhabitants of America! Should this page escape its destined conflagration at the Year's End, and these Alphabetical Letters remain legible — when your eyes behold the Sun after he has ruled the Seasons round for two Centuries more, you will know that we dream'd of your Times."

It is up to all of us to cherish this dream — and make sure everybody's revolution remains the heart and soul of the story.

The surrender of the British army to the French and Americans at Yorktown in 1781 was the knockout blow that forced King George III to accept the independence of the United States.

GLOSSARY

aide-de-camp a military assistant.

boycott an agreement not to buy or use goods or services to protest a political policy. Americans organized several boycotts of imports from England.

company unit of a regiment, commanded by a captain; at full strength, ninety-one men.

Continental army a military force that consisted of soldiers from the thirteen rebelling colonies. They enlisted for three years or the duration of the war. General George Washington was their commander in chief.

Continental Congress the political body that governed the confederation of thirteen colonies in rebellion against English rule. Each colony sent a group of delegates. The president of the Congress was selected by the delegates.

dragoons cavalrymen armed with sabers as well as pistols and muskets.

Indian Nation This is the term American Indians preferred to use, rather than tribe. Each nation considered itself an independent country, like the United States.

loyalists Americans who supported King George III and English rule. More than 100,000 Americans were loyalists.

manumission The literal meaning of this word is "free from one's hand." It was used to describe the act of freeing someone from slavery.

militia civilians who served as soldiers for short periods, usually two or three months, to assist the Continental army. They were organized by the states.

minutemen militia with special training, who were supposed to respond to an emergency on a minute's notice.

Parliament the political body that ruled England, along with King George III. Parliament consisted of the House of Commons and the House of Lords. Members of the House of Commons were elected by English voters. Members of the House of Lords inherited their seats.

regiment a unit in an army, consisting of eight companies. A regiment is commanded by a colonel.

skirmish an exchange of gunfire between two small groups of armed men. Often a skirmish preceded a battle.

slaves men and women who were the property of their owners. They could be bought and sold. By the time the Revolution began, all American slaves were African Americans. In the previous century, some Indians were enslaved. Liverpool, England, was the headquarters of the world's slave trade.

FURTHER READING AND WEB SITES

FURTHER READING

Allen, Thomas B., and Cheryl Harness (Illustrator). *George Washington, Spymaster: How the Americans Outspied the British and Won the Revolutionary War*. National Geographic Society, 2004.

Cox, Clinton. *Come All You Brave Soldiers: Blacks in the Revolutionary War*. Scholastic, 2002.

Draper, Allison Stark. *What People Wore During the American Revolution*. Rosen Publishing, 2003.

Fink, Sam. *The Declaration of Independence: The Words That Made America*. Scholastic, 2002.

McCarthy, Pat. *Thirteen Colonies from Founding to Revolution in American History*. Enslow, 2004.

Moore, Kay, and Daniel O'Leary (Illustrator). *If You Lived at the Time of the American Revolution*. Scholastic, 1998.

Murray, Stuart. *Eyewitness: American Revolution*. DK Publishing, 2002.

Redmond, Shirley Raye. *Patriots in Petticoats: Heroines of the American Revolution*. Bantam Doubleday Dell Books for Young Readers, 2004.

Rosen, Daniel. *Independence Now: The American Revolution 1763-1783*. National Geographic Society, 2004.

Stewart, Gail B. *Revolutionary War*. Blackbirch Press, 2003.

WEB SITES

The Revolutionary War: A Journey Towards Freedom!
http://library.thinkquest.org/10966/index.html

The American Revolution for Kids
http://www2.lhric.org/pocantico/revolution/revolution.htm

National Park Service Museum Collections
http://www.cr.nps.gov/museum/exhibits/revwar/

Loyalty or Liberty
http://www.history.org/History/teaching/revolution/a1.html

The American Revolution Round Table of New York
http://samson.kean.edu/~leew/arrt/index.html

George Washington Papers at the Library of Congress 1741–1799
http://lcweb2.loc.gov/ammem/gwhtml/gwhome.html

Liberty! The American Revolution
www.pbs.org/ktca/liberty

Lots of Links from a Theme Unit
http://edtech.kennesaw.edu/web/amrevol.html

Free Black Patriots
http://www.pbs.org/wgbh/aia/part2/2p53.html

Women of the American Revolution
http://www.americanrevolution.org/women.html

INDEX